Drifting

Drifting

PJ Thomas

2024 PAJE Press

Published by: PAJE Press
586 Bethune Street, Peterborough, Ontario, K9H 3Z8

Editor: Sarah Perkins

Layout: Esther Vincent
Author photo: Andy Carroll

Thomas, PJ
Drifting/ PJ Thomas.
Poems.
ISBN 978-1-7772837-2-8 (paperback)
Subjects: Poetry

Acknowledgments

This book is dedicated to Frank Flynn,
for inspiring so much of the love.

Thank you to the following organizations for helping foster interest and community in poetry:

Electric City Culture Council
The League of Canadian Poets
Sadleir House Community Centre
Take Cover Books
Trent Radio
Watson & Lou
The Writers' Union of Canada

I would also like to thank these helpful people:

Charon Ackhurst
David Bateman
Rick Fines
Olivia Flynn
Mridul Harbhajanka
Laurel Paluck
Betsy Prucha
Jill Staveley
Wendy Trusler

Foreword

In the aftermath of the early '20s, no not the roaring '20s, our '20s, our relation to one another came into focus. Where do I end and you begin? Are we too far or too close? What is just right? The crevices between us where we let each other in.

As 2020 rolled in, like for many, my plans became null. A group performance project, which brought people together through PJ's poetry got postponed, then paused, then cancelled. But PJ has kept the line open, weaving, word by word, poem by poem.

As PJ's *Bottle Socializing* goes within these pages,

> "Laughing and smoking
> but never feeling
> liquid contents within"

In the aftermath, no one is unchanged, an no one around is unchanged. Where does that leave our connections to one another? What did we miss and what do we now dread? And where do we go from here...

Art is arguably the most effective form of processing and it cannot be taken away by any one or any *thing*.

Drifting explores you and me, intimate and superficial, desired and regretted, longed for and fed up with.

Welcome, reader, to a book where, poem by poem, your heart is waiting to be found,

"Strip down to your skin,
laugh and love,
and a little bit deeper in"

(PJ Thomas, *Your Death or Mine*)

- Mari Ya, a day in May 2024

Contents

Time Alone Together

We met without distraction,
no wine we could swirl in a glass
as we took our time to think,
no candle to look away and light for a second,
no dinner, no movie;
the things that would have kept me away,
or vaguely there, and looking elsewhere.
We met without a board game,
arcade, or ping pong.
We had so much to discuss
though we hadn't known each other long.
And for the first time alone together,
we were there in nature,
sitting on a log
listening to frogs
and the comforting drone of bees,
when you reached for my hand,
and I casually touched your knee.

Right Behind You

I need to hide from the zenith of the day.
Any peak is precarious,
unless like you, we teeter-totter
on the top of Mount Olympus.

You are unafraid
of your own passing,
know you have done life
with skill and caring,
know love from the dawning
and on into evening
when you kindle the fires
for mood and for warmth.

I toast you with clear champagne
from glaciers melted
into the cup of good cheer.
Be forewarned that I don't say goodbye well.
I just ignore the oblivion
that will follow this heaven
of being in your wake.

She Will Lift You Up

I saw her today
at the cafe.
There was no one else there,
so we could sit long,
basking in curved wooden chairs
that wrapped around our backs.
Our conversation came easy.
Empathy and humour will do that.
We practice the way
of trying to do a right thing.
There is an optimal outcome
for any situation,
striving for harm reduction
in all our dealings.
Relationships are tantamount
to my heartbeat.
I require mutual harmony at almost any cost.
And she needs truth, honour and justice
for squirrels, loved ones
and drug-addicted folks
who have fallen in the street.

Naked Infinity

There's a sink load of dishes
but I want to write you
a love letter so long
it will never end
until all the drops of the ocean,
and every speck of sand
lying on the beach,
falls away,
and, left naked
as our first day,
we stare into the abyss of scars
and fractures, and severances;
quick cuts from the mother,
the wine cellar, the beauty boutique.
You saw the light of day
glowing on my partner's skin
as she was lying there,
without a care beyond the confines
of a finite world.

The Cards We're Dealt

I feel your heartstrings,
pulled-tight
tethers across your brow,
convoluted furrows of meaning.
Lines around your eyes and chin
are etched by time alone,
carving tracks
through repetition
and unfounded premonitions:
deep and final.
Do we all get our fair share
of sweet and bitter?
Must we accept our lot in life;
this strange, lop-sided mix
of sunshine and rain?

Float

I rise in the still-dark.
Early quiet marches across my head.
I miss your wit and our magic.
You are engaged and focused.
I let loose and float,
coast,
keep tiptoe on the crest of waves
that come and go.
I need to keep it light
and ride on moonbeams
that touch the water
and move it closer,
depending when and where you are.
I am searching celestial things,
like when my heart energy zings
with our humour and grace.
I am almost always sad
no matter what's going on.
We have known old hurts,
bear wounds that will not close.
That's why I cannot delve and duck
below the waves.
So, I am also always happy,
and know that this is all temporary,
anyways.

Archetype of Love

You jump over the trip wires,
constantly playing castanets in your head.

Fortune smiled upon you
and gave you a big toothy grin,
put money in your wallet,
and some fair winds in your sails.

Here, the branches are bare,
frozen fog hanging in the streetlights,
a glow around the face of the moon.
It's enough to have a cup of tea
and think a moment
looking out the window
at the pitch-black of the night.

I collect myself,
put a better spin on things.
I need to let you go,
drop my hopes that we would be close
though I never had you,
never wanted you pinned to a display card
but to spread your living wings.
I like my sweet ideas of you,
and you fit the bill so well.
I dreamt you before I met you,
then you turned out to be much more.

Fall into Tomorrow

Quiet tonight,
silent streets.
Just the rain
typing on the drainpipe.
A car drives by and I am jarred.
This is such a holy time,
after your honest opinion,
holding a communion
of what we find pleasing.
No tomorrow
trespasses on today,
but, like a cat at a mouse hole,
it waits for you to walk
through the portal
and to be swallowed
way down
its spiralling throat.

Let's Spend Time

How did you slip
into such immediate importance,
get top rotation on my brain radio station?
I play our seeming songs over in my head,
so far, a few vignettes
without much yet said.

I want to soon bask
in the wry light of your smile,
see my name shaped on your lips,
spit with tenderness
from out of the raw quiet.

No one knows what will go on here
except we two
between our tete-a-tete,
this late evening rain,
and the morning silence.

Dim Today

I'm turning on all my lights
at high noon.
Singing, screaming, and shrieking
your name
in a whisper that falls away
like a feather;
soft and easing down.
I want a few things from you
and they are exactly
a big loving hug,
your warm, warm hand on mine,
to hear you tell me
not to be captured
by fear alone,
irrational beliefs,
or erroneous thinking.
You are my grounding wire,
my strong anchor chain
when the monsoons of torrential rain come in.
We have at least a spring to go,
you and I,
some grey and blue skies to see,
and to meet again the month of May,
when I first laid eyes on you.

Love Poem

Scrap that. That was trash.
I scratch out letters and lines,
edit, erase, and rearrange by design.
Nothing can be read
unless it's a word first,
or perhaps a sigh,
or the corners of your mouth
turned down or tilting up,
in a slow smile, or abrupt frown.
It doesn't matter now,
because we are just clowning around
this crazy thing called love.
So, if I don't write it right,
describe my heart
with artistry and humour,
will you give me a pass
to just like you a lot?
Because that's all I've got anymore.

I Have Lost You

That was the first time I saw you
and didn't fall in love again.
It was just ho hum.
I felt like I didn't want
to know more of you,
like picking up a good book
that you can't put down.
You were less familiar than ever,
like you were a nice stranger
who seemed pretty okay.
You have retreated
back into your good life
of family and friends,
and I need to build mine;
keep coming out
from under this rock,
find my connections
among the brave
and the few.

Cool Honey

You have stuck in my craw,
my honey lamb who prickles;
bristling, from my way-too-much love.
You, Sam and Miss Lucy
are dry-peck people
by way of a kiss,
whereas, I might give you
a juicy long bite,
linger with my cheek against yours,
twirl my fingers in your hair
and hold you so close
our hearts feel one another's beats.
But I can let you go,
my sweet sugar bear.
I never get so hung up that it hurts.
Maybe a dull, long ache
that things are not right,
or could be better
or even celebratory.
But I am used to not getting enough
from the stingy love my mother has shown.
I guess it hurt more than I let on.

Your Death or Mine

Strip down to your skin,
laugh and love,
and a little bit deeper in,
feel the pressure points of relief,
releasing energy.
You are so inclined to be free,
everybody's Handsome Ned,
friend to the fallen, and the mighty,
father to the magic of your daughters.
You are smarter than your body,
though dancers have clever images
of life, dynamism, movement, freedom.
But you know where you live,
and it is in intellect, rationale,
artistry and logic.
Your practiced philosophy
of letting go through humour,
the radical acceptance
of how the world turns
whether we want it to or not,
and how you know
your heart will never be the same again,
allows you to exist, and even thrive
through pain.
And oh, how I love you,
and will one day cry
when I have to let you go.

Bottle Socializing

If I could reach out from this tomb
of beer-bottle socializing,
break the glass and touch you,
I would be left without shelter,
vulnerable on the carpet of shattered fragments,
wounded by my courageous triumph,
oh, so happy.

But the rules of the game
are not played that way.
We must stay capped within,
under tension and pressure, yet safely contained.
Side by side,
bottles stacked,
nearly touching,
but only bottle socializing.
Laughing and smoking
but never feeling
liquid contents within;
the bubbles and the bittersweet.
If only my Id could run free
for a few precious moments,
I could break the glass
and we could puddle together.
Pools in the cup of freedom.

Mail Call

You carry my thoughts away
to the far reaches of questioning,
and I like that.
Except when focus
goes out of my brain...
Why was I writing to you?
I can't remember now
the screen has changed to Gmail,
and there you are,
sending back love
in that warm-hearted way you have,
like you're christening every moment
with blessings acquired over a lifetime;
sprinkling your brand of fairy dust,
the light of star-quality,
and buttercup pollen
the colour of sunshine
always under the chin.
I want no more from you
than what you can lend,
freedom and support to a friend,
love that will see one of us
through to the fatal end,
though I feel like I'll live forever,
since right before I met you,
when we were just writing letters.

March First

Today, I'm going to let time slide.
We begin anew at the end of winter.
Something is waking inside me
like the green leaf erupts
from the frozen twig.
It's all coming soon;
the close sunlight,
walking freely instead of hurrying,
scurrying home before we perish
in the cold wind.
I want blue grass on the hills
hosting sheep and lambs,
and it turns out, I will soon get it
unless the end comes before
the next beginnings.
Are we moving into war?
We are all neighbours here on Earth.
What can we do to help each other
find our groove?
I let time slide.
The sun is rising.

My Best New Friend

It's okay if it's not okay,
if you haven't adjusted
to the cracked sky
and fallen angels.
I can only lift your hand to my face
and offer you
the grace of friendship;
of a kind of love eternal
that has no answers,
with nothing expected in return.
We can hold close to nature,
walk with each other in chilly winter
not just the sweet spring
when the river runs smooth and easy.
I'll meet you on the new moon
of the new year
and we can tell each other
where we have been,
and where we might like to go.

Not Never

Words worrying the page,
frightening, exciting,
something to get worked up about.
It doesn't take much,
just my ideas of your face
gracing the mind's photo album.

I can picture
all kinds of stories;
long tales, and short regales
of laughter.
Let tomorrow wait forever
teetering on the brink
of when I will see you again.

It's all okay
as this night rotates into day.
One more sun
till next we meet.
Could I wait again
for a lifetime?
And here you come late,
but not never,
after I've shuttered the windows,
and locked the doors.

Roots and Veins

Cheer up,
calm down,
lift off,
come around
to hearing the soundless symphony
of nature's quiet songs.
The melodies
of trees
beyond the wind,
singing to one another;
parents, offspring,
sisters and brothers
are whispering pulses underground,
holding each other.

Starting

How did I get this far already?
To the high end of light
where refracting patterns,
prisms and lit matchsticks,
Day-Glo brightness
with full colours for fanfare
are streaming out behind our heads,
and all we have said
to one another
is so small a percentage
of what has occurred.
Is it meant for us to talk for hours?
Catch up
on our past mistakes and bright ideas,
forgotten clandestine moments,
tears of terror and of sadness.
Lost for a time of wondering
which way do we go
from here?
But I do not despair
at the lateness of our time.
We are just starting to know each other
and the sky has been hinting to the stars
that you would show up here
at home in my backyard.

Timely Embrace

Indelible illusion,
like a see-through tattoo
high on a bosom.
Your heart, there like that,
as we touch chest to chest and chat.
I like your meaning.
When I first saw you with the dancer,
my heart warmed with her beauty.
I'm happy, it's true.
Does she want all of you?
Will she lay claim to your heart
like so many women do?
I see single women swarm
my recently-single male friends
with casseroles, and cleaning,
care that's half maternal concern,
mixed with a want to be with them
and make them burn with desire.
I like to laugh with the men.
It's all I've ever wanted to do
until I met you,
now that I'm so old my passion
is flannel hugs, sharing tea,
and describing to each other
how we came to be.

If

You don't know me,
don't know all the shameful and shining
things I have done.
But I want to know more of you.
Is it dangerous to my heart
for you to capture my interest,
my intrigue, and affinities all?
I can turn them on and off like a light switch,
but at what cost?
A falsehood to my calloused heart
to laugh and say it's okay
when it isn't
and probably won't ever be.
Is that negativity bias?
Are we made to make each other
feel welcome, joyous, and free?
I have no idea who I want to be to you;
friend, poet, advisor, truth seeker?
But I know I want to soak you up,
breathe you in,
absorb some of your essence
through psychic osmosis
without being a vampire,
and while always wanting the very best to be.
Your happiness would delight me.

Where the River Meets the Lake

At the height of summer,
when the water doesn't run cold
and cicadas and crickets rule the evenings,
I think of sandpipers on beaches
ringing their whistled calls.
We are all in symphony,
running in tandem,
all cause-and-effect
with the ebb and flow
of our energies wrought by sunlight.
You brighten my day
in all the strongest ways,
like rays of bright shine
gleaming off the lake.
The river runs through my heart
and pours out into the bay.
Boats bob on small waves
in this protected harbour.
The geese are feeding on the grass.

Collecting Light

The freedom of bliss
is like the kiss of the moon.
It bestows gifts
upon those who partake
of midnight dances.
Chances taken to say I love you
are so rarely a mistake.
That song is a refrain
we want to hear again and again,
when it's ringing clear and true.
I want to give something dear to you,
something shiny and new
like tomorrow's burgeoning sunrise
glittering with surprises.

One Day at a Time

Time on my own
with just a notepad and pen.
I sketch the weather
with your face in the clouds.
But my words are wrung out
like Monday morning's wash
and are soon hung to dry.

Creaking sobs from my dusty throat
are not enough to convince me
that I really am sad.
What it is, is more like floating
around a lightning core;
detached yet not disconnected,
so happy that I met you,
like a moth to the flame,
as though for a while
I could never be sad again.

You are alone in your mirror.
You keep combing out your tresses,
hoping they will tame.
But I know the wild boar
that is your head,
the stubborn mule
in the kick of your leg,
the black panther tracking game
in the tricky fiction of your heart.
You have no need to fear.
Each day we start again
with the supposition
that we want to be friends.

Precious

You are a rare stone,
something a person can find
maybe once in a lifetime.
But you were already found,
discovered, revealed as bounty.
A wishing stone,
you gave something back
from a very young age.
I live in the twilight,
in shadows long at the end of day.
I will hint at goodbye now
and let my heart rip.
It's okay.
I wasn't wanting more from you,
just to revel in your brightness.
Shiny and smooth
without rough edges,
polished by the tumbling seas
as a gift of love that came to be
resting on these shores
for such a brief while.

Swift and Smart

Open the craters of the moon.
Fly fast into the wings, harps,
the heartstrings of angels,
humming, playing,
crying just to be heard.
Come with me over the hill
to the rainbow fields
where new hay waits soon
beneath the surface of this land;
the rolling ground,
where magnetism runs deep.
I saw irises today
springing forth in green spears
up out of last year's brown grasses and weeds.
Tufts of kelly-coloured turf
gather around the well,
getting extra spilled water
and thus, flourish and thrive.
Let me stand next to you
to soak up your sunshine,
dive into the continuous rivers
that flow from your eyes,
the depths of your being,
where humour and warmth
are brought forth almost daily.
We keep constantly moving forward
because we have no choice
but to go into the light.

We Meet on George Street

I ran smack dab into you.
Our hearts smashed together.
There was warmth and contentment;
you hugging me, cradled to your centre,
and we stood like that
on the busy sidewalk,
the cars flashing past.

Friendship knows no bounds of adult ego,
can touch you on the forehead,
tickle you about your middle,
tingle up your spine
when it's clever.

We are cracking up
and telling each other truths
about our dark side,
our demons packed in baggage
that maybe now we can set by the curb.
The taxi cab comes to collect me,
and I leave the luggage behind.

Good to Know You

For some reason, I want to shriek
until the windowpanes shake,
rant and rave to no one here.
But I keep quiet, try to be silent.
The landlords are just downstairs
and who wants to overhear
as someone implodes?
Not I, because looking way up high
is all I know how to do,
to keep smiling into stormy skies,
and sigh when the moon breaks through
the velvety blue of this night.
I am usually alright alone,
keep a bright way of looking at things
as a defense against my doldrums;
worse than tempests,
or serpents on the sea.
But tonight, I want to be with you
to ask you questions,
listen to your tirades,
bask in knowing
that you are traveling along with me,
and I am not really alone,
but can live in your thoughts as home.

Midnight Conversation

When I think of New Year's Eve,
I think of shine;
iridescent bubbles of oil slick prisms,
sparkle, spangle, tingles of glistening
snowflakes on lashes,
a mountain of lace
on your bright red hair.

I think tweet, honk, holler;
taxis leaning on the horn,
yellow lights flashing,
catching caution from the wind.

We go when we see the green,
laughing, taking each other's arms
as a group of partiers
on a pub crawl at midnight.
We see people we know,
revelers rollicking down the streets
for appointments with a barkeep.

But this year, it's going to be quiet;
a deck of cards and a dram of liqueur,
and you, always you
in some form, appearing...
You were ten years younger then,
and now here you are.

Here, we found grace by the duck pond,
lessons planted in last year's garden
taking root,
preparing to sprout shoots and leaves
and flowers of paperwhites.

We type languidly,
talk a little in between rhymes;
murmurs mention nuances of loveliness
in harmonious, interesting phrases.

In Real Life

Are your blushes information?
Quick lessons on reaction;
the mood in any moment.
The kind twinkle in your eye
and pursed lips blooming pink
and crimson
are reflected in the flames
on the wet tea glass.

This fire holds the heart of home...
Without it, we are empty.
And to be by the water,
feels smooth in winter,
cool in summer.
These elements are essential parts of the planet,
give rise to natural actualities
of our existence on Earth;
the place where spirit meets substance,
and the material greets the ethereal
in a dance interface of amazing grace.

And I just want to be here with you,
to see that tinge of silver in your hair,
the twitch at the corner of your lip,
that lift to your left eyebrow,
the crinkling around your smile.

The Start of a Simple Day

I'll get up early and bake for you
Saturday morning cookies
with oats and brown sugar.
Have a cup of coffee and warm to the day.
Skip the news and start slow.
Hear the birdsong out in the cold
as the setting moon
knows just where to lay her head,
rolling in low heavens
that slide slowly below the horizon.
And on the other side,
the sun rises in the east,
quiet along the shoreline
where ducks that have not left
cluster around the banks.
Let's sit out in the sun
as the wind whistles up off the lake.
Our coffee steams in the morning light.

Arriving

Did you reach the evening sun?
Make it to the beach
before the day was done?
Lay yourself out, long and stretched,
and then dive...
Leap from the dock into the drink
like your life depended on it.
Swim out past the rocks,
beyond the shoals
that keep you close to harbour.
Go farther and farther
till you have one last breath
before turning back.
Then glide on your side
in a slow resting stroke,
getting closer to home.
I see you in my mind's eye
arise from the waters that undulate endlessly,
pushing you in towards land.
Your cabin faces west,
and the sun is soon to set.

Come Along

I'm walking off into mysteries,
night fog swirling, clouding the moon.
Would you like to get lost with me?
One more quick turn around a corner
and we won't know where we are.
Searching the dark space between us,
looking for a landmark,
something familiar,
someplace we recognize.
This wonder is new to me,
and I may seem a little confused.
But I know you,
can trust your voice
even when I can't see your mouth.
I can hear your smile beginning
as you speak,
sounding peaceful and calm,
kind and reflective,
thoughtful without telling me
what I already know.

Dance in the Winds of Change

You keep dancing,
tippy-toe across the tightrope.
Shuffle kick and the old soft shoe,
you know the routine;
keep moving by rote
when inspiration runs thin.
You have managed to choreograph joy
into your life,
have cried with your whole body,
all of your being wrapped up in the sword dance
of dangerous living.
I have finally learned to move peaceably
between the shards of shattered expectations.
Specific longings always crack and break.
They are too static and brittle.
We need to be more open
to fate's interpretations
of getting what we need.
But I will never know better
than to want, to hope.
I keep lifting my head to see the real me
in the razzmatazz of life's sweet abandon.
Am I too busy searching for the forest
to see the trees swaying?
I could be enlightened
by my amusement with movement,
enthralled by your each and every turn.

Moving Along

Don't remind me of when I was sad,
but tell of my brightest shining moment;
that time when I felt most open and free,
realizing what you mean to me,
and what we will come to be.

Chime in about a Christmas past
when all we could do was laugh
because the dog chewed all of our presents.
There was my new china doll
with her hair all matted and gnarled.
That enthusiastic cur
ripped my handknit mittens,
and the slipper socks were covered in slobber
and chewed into knots of dropped stitches
from their patterns of purple clover.

Remind me of that time I was brave enough
to leap off the dam
into the cascading water,
screaming all the way down
because my lungs couldn't keep a secret
from the heart in my chest.
They were posing a question
of what to breathe
on the other side of the surface
of the river water rippling,
flowing stridently above.

Transposed

There is something mostly
in the realm of beauty
about your personage.
You float through my transom;
of the world, but not in it.
You lie at my feet and look up
and I can only feel
sunshine beaming down between the clouds,
light rain on a warm breeze,
cold frost for excitement,
and fireside heat for pleasing.
We know mutual admiration,
and when you are no longer a body,
but an idea,
no longer under the skies,
but perhaps in and above them,
let me look to you for love,
for your suggestions and notions,
for your suppositions,
and hints at possibilities.
Let me find you within;
warm in the caverns of my mind
where you can romp and play
until I am out of days,
existing only in a ray of sunshine
and the minds of those who know me.

Life Drawing

Love is uncomfortable;
like a porcupine on your pillow,
his quills up and down your spine;
like a gorilla in your tea shop
smashing all the dishes.
It twists, and it twirls you,
whirling around its mixed boys and girls,
collecting like a cluster of clowns
set loose on the downtown.
And we wake up and it's all painted red.
Purple passion hurls us
up and down the rollercoaster,
traveling faster than our fears.
And no one can quite catch up to us
because now we can fly
like stringless kites in the sky.
Drift by on pinkish clouds,
your mounds lying in all the right places.

Consciousness

Things are pretty good in here.
I found the sunshine of my mind
in an empty room.
The gods give me what they want;
dribs and drabs and all the greatest gifts
mixed up with some mayhem,
and a sense of order and place.
I want to thank them forever
for one moment here with you,
the grace of dragonflies and buttercups,
fresh snow under the moon,
your canoe gliding quietly
across an autumnal lake.
Will you ever forsake me?
Erase my memory,
or all of yours of me,
from our early days,
to the someday-coming ending.
All that is, and has been
in between
is a flash of biology
and the psychic pulse of the sun.
Or does it just flow on,
this invisible life,
our indivisible love?
The days are running into a springtime
of irises and wild roses.
Is there any time to rest
along the way?

First Tryst

My searchlight gaze
skims the surface of your eyes;
their shining, ever-changing colours.
I look deeper
and all your emotions
are explained in your lights
like sapphires lit for night time,
burning even brighter
when you start your good-natured lying.

And after all our vanity
is burned to ash
and the morning sun
flashes rapidly between clouds,
we will walk each other close to home
and linger long in the garden.
We say goodbye many times,
touch our fingertips together,
intrigued by our twists of fate.

Full Moon with You

They run from start to finish,
these half-spun tales
and verses of visions.
Can you see the colours in the crystals
dangling in my moonlit window?
I spin the thread
of prism discos,
see the rainbows on your face,
and across the grace of light,
the arc of joy falls from your eyes.
Let's put our tears away in a treasure chest
with the years of yearning
for one spark to catch;
to light the flames of magic in our minds,
burning rose-tinted candles
in our covenant of the divine.

The Line of the Horizon

Quiet morning
on the porch in the light.
Waves of white
undulate slowly
across the arc of sky.

I see your face
up in the clouds
streaked by the wind,
and wonder if you are sleeping
or tossing and turning,
looking for truth and learning
in the skills of a free fall.

You are digging below the horizon
for roots, and deep springs,
great gaping pools,
and wells of sweet water.
I believe I've seen
the flash of your being.

Heartbeat

I've been the cruelest at the game of life
and the kindest known to humans.
I ran the rat race for half my life,
stumbled out from under treatment.
I found the real world full of folly,
summoned love by simply calling to it.

You led me to your living room at night;
it was warm, the glass doors were open.
We peered at the moon,
and five stars in parallel,
looking forward while talking in turns.
We were side by side and listening
to the music of the spring peepers
and birds of the night;
standing in the gleam of Luna,
hearing each other and the great wide world.
I whispered close to your beating chest.
Is there anything more alluring
than secret knowledge?

I always need to re-think my ego
and stop fanning the flames of its vanity.
I say, rest easy, worried self,
because you are enough.
You are truly okay as you are.
Keep striving for improvement,
but find peace in between.
Do not hide in the quiet, but seek solace.
Find moments of utter stillness
while the blood keeps flowing,
and the heart is pumping.

After Sundown

"I feel too soft and sad," she said.
And then she added,
"why the endless I, I, I?
I tell myself to shut up about it.
No one cares on Saturday night
that there's a lonely old woman
locked up in her room,
afraid to go out or venture far."

She needs to be alone and it's okay, she says.
"Not great. Just kind of fine."

People are partying, and drinking,
and smashing bottles
out back in the alley
behind her window.
She sits inside in quiet,
happy to be home, but lonely for him.
They would laugh about the neighbours,
and steer clear of the darkness.

Honey, My Friend, Listen

You make me radiate, vibrate, percolate;
smiles and chuckles,
belly laughs and big guffaws,
tickles and giggles.
I feel so immediate,
like the fast flame
from striking a match.

I sense in you
your internal electric ignition,
your impulse, imagination,
instinct, intuition.
We spark up in humour.

You exude dazzling wit,
the physical comedy
that comes to you naturally,
and your pleasant expressions of face.
What I love about you most
becomes your blazing intelligence.
But it will be okay
when good minds falter.
They do that sometimes.

All of your gifts, blessings, and ruins
have made you a kinder, wiser person.
I feel waves of calm
emanating from your character,
like sunshine from a bee.

Lift Off

I'm giving my boyfriends away.
Would you like one of them?
There's the one that delivers milk.
We mix it with honey,
let it flow mellow around the cup.
His name is Isaiha; he is amazing.

There's the one who raises tadpoles
and plays with salamanders.
We drift around the pond
looking for frog eggs
among the green fronds.
His name is Horace, he is a green biologist.

Then, there's the one named Steve.
He races Formula One with champion speed.
He smells a bit like axel grease.
He knows how to pleasure a woman
and tease the willing men.
Cheeky, with his leather suit and fenders.

And my favourite guy,
I can't let go to you,
though he might want to.
He's clearing out my closets
to make room for living,
getting rid of the old coffins of skeleton bones.
Him, I would marry, as my very best friend,
but on our last day alive.
We'd take a breath, a kiss, and say goodbye.

Carry On

Let's go to the beach
and forget time--
except for that divine sweep of sky
telling us if we need to sleep.

The dampness of morning
greets the dear, dreary dawn.
We see the mist collected on a silver fox,
the fog hanging over the lake.

All I need is to reach
your sunny warm hand to hold,
my friend, my partner,
to feel all is well and good.

Night falls and the stars are visible,
tingeing the sky with excitable light
well after the fact.
I've heard some stars are gone now,
but still, they shine on down to us
in billions of years of wondrousness.

For My Lovely

We travel at the speed of light.
I have let my hopes of you go
back to the sun,
the solar system from which we come,
the cosmos of a quagmire of love.
We are friends,
but if I didn't have to be
rubbed and naked and mounted,
I would want to marry you
for your Dyson vacuum cleaner,
your winning personality,
the way you always come up smarter
than my greatest expectations.
You are kindly in your mind.
I am always underestimating
your magnificent capacity for love.
It is real because
you have tapped into the infinite
as your wellspring source,
your starting point,
the great beginnings we are all made of.
You come from always-good intentions.
Bask in them joyfully.

Inkling

I know where secret things hide;
in the creases of your brow,
the flutter of your heart,
in your dreamy faraway eyes.
You are remembering
all the beautiful moments of life;
treaties between your heart and mind
not to cast away brightness,
the gentle lightness of the air,
or the aspirations of hope
and a sound mind.
I am an amplifier of emotion,
see things bigger than they appear
in my rearview mirror.
Sure, that was then,
but it is also always now...
Every moment rolled into one;
the sum total of experience.

Whether or Not

Either something will happen,
or it won't.
It doesn't matter
in the larger scheme of things.
Did you pick up your new shoes
from the cobbler,
or the posies at the florist?
If you wash your clothes
today or tomorrow,
will it make a difference
to next Tuesday?
No one is more scared
than you or me,
and still our confidence blossoms.
We keep moving through and into
higher realms of consciousness,
you know, where buttercups drip,
and music plays from a leaf,
and we run into the sunrise
as it comes to meet us.
And if I'm there
a moment before you,
I will pave the heavens
with red rose petals.

I Want Your Conversation

I was just in the kitchen
trying to think of a reason to call.
But I realized we are way past pretense.
I've already told you, I love you,
a hundred times this year.
I'm sure it's okay to say,
I'd like to talk to you,
want to get evermore understanding
of who you are.
The hurts, the aches, the angst;
let them slide past the sides of my head.
Your small and great joys will go noted
into my memory vault of treasures,
here now, perhaps gone from me someday.
And maybe one day I'll be a hero;
save the town from a flaming train,
provide a meal and a warm bed,
remember every blessed thing you said.

By Fire and Water

Come to a place
where we can crash on the shore,
wake up on damp sand
by a fire pit
where we burned even the marshmallow sticks.
Did we dance and howl around the flames
at a certain time
when the moon was rising?
I remember sitting quietly
at 4:00 in the morning,
your hand holding mine,
and wondering is there anything
more sublime, divine
than an ocean beach
with the whales breaching
up through the channel?
It is your face, your nature, your reason.

All I Have

These words will break through my surface
to become notes out into the world
about love and pain,
gain and loss,
the ups and downs of our dual nature.
I am the extremes,
and you are the nuances
of subtle things in between.

As the feather falls,
sliding away from flight,
it rides the breeze
slipping back and forth from left to right
as though delicate decisions are being made
about where and when to land perfectly.
You can feel the beauty
in its ending with the sky.
I feel loss
from soaring around the mountain tops
to lying dormant in a muddy swamp.
These things I ride with you.

But we do not stay long
floundering in the quagmire.
We become something else.
Like the phoenix, maybe we rise
and fly again in a different skin.
No longer your father's chin,
and your mother's eyes,
but I would recognize you
in any disguise.

This Place

I watch the swirling river at night
with the bridge lights shining
down on black water.
The willows by the banks
trail their thin fingers
in the stream.
Let go of your dreams for one night
and follow me
into the centre of town.
We can play hide and seek
in the dark streets,
see the water's moving patterns,
and walk through the riverside park
where each garden tells us stories
about community and history.
Hear the music
on this summer evening
playing up from the harbour bandstand.
Cast a stone into the flowing river,
and make a wish to be remembered.

Humanity

Upsy-daisy and round about,
topsy-turvy and up and down
we careen into the future.
Every present moment
glows alive
like lit candles on birthday cake.
We have found the value of our lives
in our own taunting, teasing deaths,
swung on the pendulum
till letting go to survive.
And if my heart blows up,
just throw dirt over me and laugh.
I had such a very good time
in this life;
this aching, breaking apart,
casting asunder, and getting over it
if we can.
And if not,
let drop any pretenses
that we are more than loving each other;
sisters and brothers.

Across Canada

I want to live with you
in the mountains
and on the beaches,
dry gulch prairies,
and the rainforest out west.
I can be maritime
with a sublime turn of fish;
drying salt cod on shakes
made out of birch wood.
We barely grew potatoes and carrots,
the moose ate all the cabbages.
There's not much earth to farm
on rock and bog.
I lived on a cliff
overlooking the sea,
so far and long
across the water,
my eyes squinting
at the sunlight glitter;
saw whales and icebergs
floating between our island
and the mainland,
where people talk about themselves.

I was frankly scared
in the flats of Saskatchewan;
too much sky, endless sky
immense and limitless,
and I was lost without my landmarks.
In the foothills of Alberta,
I learned of lush and rugged landscape;
a way to be soft and green,
several feet of powdered snow,
distant glacier lakes floating gently,
the ground strong in bedrock.
And you, always you,
in the start and finish of every poem.
My mind wanders back here
in the thin mountain air.

Light and Dark

The sky is grey and gold
as the universe touches us always,
holds us in layers of air and dust.
We have traveled through light years
to be here now.
This truism is no news of revelations
as we think of the clogged kitchen sink,
the stray cat beneath the back porch,
our 401k contributions,
and all the other day to day events,
occurrences, incidents that keep happening
over and over in everyone's cycle of life.
But what if we don't always react?
Let thoughts pass by peaceably
as everything falls by the wayside.
Can we focus sometimes on the keyhole of light
that shines from our third eye
like white-hot fire
into the cold black night?

There

I want to reach you, touch you, meet you.
How I laughed and felt tickled
when we laid on the dock under the stars.

The morning lake vapours look like spirits
marching towards the sun.
Let's walk hand in hand
up stoney paths and byways.

We have made the grade of loving
like the two loons breaching, fluttering,
calling to each other
from either end of the lake.

We swim out to the sand bar,
stand high above the water
while still in the deeps.

Life and death are contradictions in terms.
One day, we will not be here,
will no longer make paths
with our hungry feet.

Your Warmth Comes from Centre

I felt your hand not fluttering,
but strong against my palm.
You are neither hesitant nor lost,
but speak clearly from the centre
to the perimeter,
the equator to the polar
ends of the Earth.
Your ideas and actions,
words and deeds,
sentiments and suggestions
fall true to your path
of wandering, meandering, running boldly
around this planet.
We can only put one foot
in front of the other,
one day, next to another
for all the time
that spirals through life.
I am elated to share Terra Firma with you
as we trod across the skin
of this delicate place.

Bouillabaisse

In tonight's moment of quiet,
it's you who comes to mind.
Lately, I'm finding ducks and drakes
flying lonely
through scattered clouds
of white light and purple dark.
You are always surrounded
by those pouring out their love
into the river of your soul.
And with that holy water,
you slake our thirsty roots,
running cool and smooth
like you are Neptune in marble
carved for the Trevi Fountain.
Do all the Sirens of Titan
call to your heart?
And me from the sea hags,
laughing at you basking in your glory.
Do you occasionally haul up on land,
make a fire, and baste yourself
in the savoury drippings
of fresh meat with salt?
I still swim in brine with my eyes wide open,
hoping for dolphins
and other intelligent beings of the deeps
to seep into my dreams
and guide me, gliding
down to the sea beds of mystery.

Man About Town

He is a gadabout
who knows all the right haunts,
tips the servers well
when they bring him what he wants.
He is well-dressed and pretty,
sits upright and ready,
he knows where he's headed,
this man about town.

His leather shoes are polished,
his jacket is from college.
He knows how to promenade boldly
around the fountains, squares, and foliage.
But he meanders by the water,
truly loves his dear, sweet daughters.
I write him poems and letters,
and we laugh and cry like clowns.

I applaud his social graces.
He deserves every happiness.
So many people love him,
and some want him for their own.
But he requires his freedom,
and no one could begrudge him.
He spreads good will to all and sundry,
this man about town.

Freefalling

I like to drop like a river stone
diving back into the water where I belong.
Does the creekbed call to my minerals
with its magnetism,
some hidden force of mutual affinity?

There is no word,
no name for the emotion
that tells the truth
of what I feel for you.
No hymn of Jesus
in a sunbeam
that can quite touch my heart
and give me the lift to say,
it's okay,
it's alright...
I know someone who gets it,
comprehends the myriad of intentions
that we put behind each word.

Beyond my work,
you give me hope of heaven,
and it is a garden by the river
where we are all welcome and just.

The Great Outside

Let me find what's sleeping
at the back of the mind,
bring forth our aspirations,
fears, loves, and letting go.
Swallows make the sound of song
outside my window.
Please let me walk through the door,
down the garden path
to where I can find the trees,
cold, austere, seeming lifeless,
but I know better.
I have laid like a stone,
facedown in bed
with a head full of medicine
that didn't fix, but conquered,
slowed me down below a snail's pace,
but I knew I was alive.
Sadly, I distained the fact.
It hurt so much to turn over
my thoughts,
like a wrecking ball
kept knocking me into the shredder.
Now, I feel love somehow
in every moment of life,
and when I can't conjure it,
I remember it, or hope
for an open door
out into the wilds.

The Shine of Someone I Admire

You are helping me see
that the positive is possible
in outcomes, hopes, and dreams.
You let me be me,
with your comfort
offered in most any surroundings.
I hope we can be
cohorts in writing
our later chapters.
Does it matter now,
more than ever,
that our time is valuable,
or do we let it all
tumble and slide,
to pass our low expectations?
I want to be always striving
for the top
of whatever I'm climbing;
my Everest to your Olympus,
the great beanstalk
up to the green gods,
or the Peace Bridge
connecting us as near neighbours.
I want to always fall somewhere
within your favour.

Forever

When you're so sad,
your eyes ache in your head,
lay yourself down by my side.
Let me stroke the soft hair
on your temples
with my smooth flat hand.
We have all felt loss,
from the cricket in a jar
when we are five,
to our grandmas, maybe gone,
our friend's father
passing away in one breath.
Why do love and death
so often hold hands?
These things sometimes
become ripe together,
peak at the same time,
in the growing vines of our hearts,
the veins within our arms,
the sinews of our muscles,
like blood, and energy and stone.
If a rock can live
for a billion years,
till it is ground down to sand,
eroded into a pith of minerals,
made into dust again,
will we still be friends
at the end of the sun?

New Love

Is Jimmy having sex
this very Saturday morning?
Lollygagging among the pillows.
We hope so for him
and that he is held in love:
new romance with the late spring's blossoms.
Soon the peonies will open full;
like the lotus flower,
the water lily,
roses the colour of blood.
Jimmy looks so happy lately,
beaming, gleaming, creaming his jeans.
He whistles when he walks,
and stops by to charmingly talk
with old women at the laundry
washing yesterday's lovers
from their sheets.
I remember touching
so many years ago
now,
when the day was filled
with thoughts of the other.
I wonder how we got anything done,
mooning about spooning with our beloved?

The Last Warm Rain

The last warm rain of 2023
is falling like pearl drops,
milking the tears of a year gone by.
The sky is such a tiny bit older.
We live straddling the river;
minnows and sunfish on your side of the bay,
ducks and geese clamouring around the dam.
I could throw a stone the whole mile
to your house,
and it would hit your metal roof
like this relentless rain.
I could send a lightning bolt
from here to British Columbia
to the centre of your brain
and you would know what I was thinking.
I practice being sad and in love
like the alpha and omega.
You are free.
I am bound by feeling
I can't define;
want to pat the side of your cheek,
and kick you in the ass.

I love you no matter what,
and I really don't care who knows,
don't care if you marry my best friend,
go to jail for tax evasion,
fall off the wagon,
roll in the grass with Mary Magdalen.
But I know you will do none of these things.
You have transcended space and time
and lived to tell the tale.
I will always wish you well.

Second Sight

If I run out of my body,
could I ride with you sometimes?
Float there in your memory
though I no longer have a hide.
And if I use up all my matches
would you offer me a light?
See me in your mind's eye
like we both have second sight.

We are given so many heartbeats,
a limited number from one to when.
Don't waste them all with worry
as we swing around life's bend.
We're long-distance travelers
hoping for truth, love, and beauty.
Looking under river rocks,
researching our life stories.

Will you tell me tomorrow
what you can't say today?
Or have I always known
that you felt this way?
Happy on your own
and glad to be beside me.
Free enough to roam,
then home for toast and tea.

So, if I leave before you;
close the door on time and breathing,
will you remember I adore you
and that you gave my life a deeper meaning?
Keep a candle in the window
burning long into the night.
See me in your mind's eye
cause we both have second sight.

How Far

Thinking of you,
out on the long highway
with miles between us
as you go the distance.
And I am at home,
knitting, weaving,
sewing up loose ends
to begin our matching dresses.

I might see you in the winter
if the avalanches don't hinder you,
and the hinterland
doesn't swallow you whole.
Shall I make holiday jam
to remember your mother?
Will you bring me a stone
from the ocean shore?

And landlocked, I sit here,
baking, and making clothes.
Sometimes, I write a poem
as a way to enjoy our home,
and to think of you far away
wherever you are roaming.

I Love/Please Wear Socks

I love my motorcycle;
her sexy lines
and elegant shine
make my mind gush.
I love my tea glass
infused with rose and amber water.
I love my plant, Ferny.
He looks like the hair
of Sideshow Bob.
I adore his leafy frills,
his brown spots,
and light-green new growth.
I love the crook of your toes;
their pink and umber nails,
and unique kind of jam
in a summer running shoe.
I love the liquid look
in animals' eyes.
I love your wide, gaping smile,
because you always mean it.

Anniversary

When your sweat and salt grow sour,
stale, and too pungent,
will I remember the flowers of May?
The wild roses in June,
and crisp air of January
smiling in sunshine
over oceans of blue snow.

When our love was new
there was nothing too good for you.
I would move mountains,
lasso the moon
if the mood took you
to dine with fine silver.
I would shine up memories
and serve them on a platter
with hopes and wishes and dreams.
But now richer,
this love means more
than new patten leather boots
or springtime parades.

Today, the timbre of your voice
is like many geese screaming.
The way you're tapping your pen,
and shaking your foot,
and singing off key,
makes me want to leap out of this window,
and plummet into oblivion;
which must be so much nicer
than eternity across our table for two.
But I wouldn't trade it,
our forever love,
not for all the promise of tomorrow,
not for heavens above.

Clearing

Bringing things into focus
can be too sharp sometimes.
In the blurry fringes,
I can dream.
If the contrast is too stark,
it looks like a math problem
instead of a love poem.
And I can grow tired of love,
like the next guy,
when it's too mushy,
muddled in feelings
that can go by the wayside
like all the other cares.
And I can stop wishing
for things I don't really want.

Local Geography

How is everything?
How are you and your daughters
on the other side of the river?
I think the water connects us;
flowing Otonabee
where communities meet
around the lakes and streams.
We form one;
all of humanity, nature, the cosmos
linked together here in the valley
where cedars and otters
coexist in beauty, harmony, and symbiosis.
We are gifted to be living
on fertile land
with many beasts and trees.
I ask, please, let's not ruin it
with our pollution.
Picture future generations
running through the leaves.

Time to Leave You Alone

Did I offend you with my joking?
I tried everything to get you to laugh.
You just ghosted me.
Humour doesn't always
come across in a text.
You missed my wry smile,
the sarcastic lilt in my voice,
the quizzical tilt of my brow.
I wanted to uplift you,
help you feel better
with a giggle.
But I think I may have upset you,
and if so, I am sorry.
I always want to leave you laughing,
and to greet you with love.

Saint Nicholas on the Beach

I see ice glistening on pine
and it reminds me of you last winter
when you flew to Antigua
to be near the sea.
You and the sand
sifting through the tides'
rising and retreating
like the oscillating heartbeat
of the moon
pounding on the beach.
You told me of the waves
breaking and rolling;
water mixing quickly with air
in the tumult--
the breathing of the sea.
I saw you there in my mind's eye,
swirling turquoise water up to your knees,
and the sun was setting behind you,
giving you a halo.

Turning

He was my John the Baptist
for falling in love.
He was then the shiniest one,
stole my heart,
but he foretold of a love that's coming
just around the bend,
down the pike,
waiting for the light
on the next corner.
He wanted the best for me,
and that was the key.

I will one day twirl and release myself,
snap my fingers,
and change my mind, just like that.
Drop the hot potato
of falling in love for the first time,
twice,
and glory in knowing
that people are generally nice
wherever you go.

I can fall in love
with coniferous trees,
ponds and brooks,
rolling rocks, and reading nooks.
Let the waves of plenty
wash over me.
Set me free
from the want of your love,
or let me grow;
get to know someone else
and myself
along with you.

The Same Grace

I want to be outside,
open the windows wide.
Walk out the front door,
and our breath will rise
on fresh, free air.
We share atoms and molecules
with outer space.
I've inhaled the cells and tissues
of deer,
the sinews of squirrels
co-mingling with my strong back.
I want the silt of birds' feathers
filtering through sunlight
to land on my lashes.
Taste the moon rocks and Mars
paving our palettes
all the way to the brain.
And what of the plants
and green grasses,
the mushrooms of splendour?
In the duckweed,
the geese swim as one,
and the universe calms and pleases our eyes.

Bards I Have Known and Loved

Like a prof teaching the Classics
for fifty years,
not much has changed on my bookshelf.
Ulysses still flows
the way only Irish writers can,
paradise is lost once more,
the bowl flew right by
the catcher in the rye.
My hat is off, and, bowing,
I pay maximum respect to those
who twirl my cerebral fluid
into a swirling tickle,
and twist my lips into their warm smile
just from reading the fortune
of their clever words.

Devotion

The sheep bleat
on the side of the hill.
Ice sheets slide and shift,
break and fall away
telling tales of new lambs.
A hint of green
to believe in the coming
of something glorious;
that is, once we reach it.
We never know who
we're going to die beside.
It could be you, or them, or her.
I hope I am alone
with your face in mind,
and Lucy's psychic hand
soft in mine.

Empty Honeycomb

No longer is he serving love
like syrup from the fire.
He has turned off the tap,
shut the trap door,
closed the damper on the chimney
so the bats move back to the belfry.

I am alone so often
and usually enjoy it;
long nights making phonics
and rhythms
that sound like music;
images that make us sigh or weep,
our separate laughter thundering
like steeplechase hooves in the sky.

I wonder why,
and sometimes, it comes to me
that the fruit can ripen on the tree,
and fall down to the soil
to seed next year's spring.
So, it's alright
that he doesn't love me today.
He might again sometime,
in another way.

The Centre of the Lotus

Open your palm
just a touch,
let me see
up your arm
to your heart,
follow the meridian
from the centre
of your hand
to your perfect brain.
I want to sit there a while
in your being,
not basking,
just still for a moment,
and upright
from my spine,
to my best wishes for you.

I Love Him More

He is sleeping
in the sun,
slowly drawing breath,
and seems peaceful.
I watch him
as he shines in the light,
stretching a paw
and snuggling deeper
in his pile of pillows.
Silent is he,
as his ears glow
bright red with blood
pumping through tiny veins;
his fine, velvet skin
alive with life force.
I want to crouch down
and stroke his warm fur,
but I will not disturb him.
Let him float and meditate
in cats' dreams
that last most of the day.
It is balm for my soul
just to be near him.
I wonder
how much further
can love go?

Water Alive

The splash of the rapids
resets our hearts, puts them to rights.
And then we turn to the slow,
steady ease of the river
meandering like a waltz downstream.
Otters and turtles swim against the current,
their tiny heads dividing the river
until a fish smacks back into the water,
and ripples their fine lines of wake.

Eventually, the rapids waterfall
down to the lake
and become the misty marshes
where the carp love to lie.
This wetland hosts kingfishers
and herons paddling along the edges
of streams, swamps, and riverbanks;
stepping with stealth,
and then, like lightning, diving
their long, thin beaks
to pull up a fish.

We swim where the water is clear,
take the canoe to the sandbar
and spend an afternoon
throwing sticks for the dogs.
They bark their fool heads off,
splashing in excitement
as the sun shines like crystals
bouncing off the surface of blue.

Your Next Book

It's alright
for you to unfurl.
Turn and
undo the wraps
of your cocoon,
unraveling gauze
till the eyes can see
your woolens drop away.
And naked as the day,
you stand gleaming and wrinkled;
a teller of tales
when you have the time and inclination.
The glow comes from within
warmth and breath
for a thin slice of forever,
slimmer than a sheet of vellum
in the composite libraries of the world.
And you sit bare atop the pages,
writing the truth on tomorrow.

Call It Another Love Poem

Thank you for triggering
the pleasure centres of my brain
with your handsome good looks.
How dare you, sir?
But I liked you in that special way
before I saw your face,
your gracefulness,
and evidence of your heart.
I was set on a path
to only write about love,
never feel it,
though it surrounds me
like a phosphorescent globe.
But you are funny and charming;
a prince without the pomp,
a warm family man,
good friend,
and valued confidante.
I wish I could feel more plainly about you,
without my heartsore vanity
and frills of hopeful poetry,
before the pills remade me
as someone I don't recognize.
But all of this combined
made me love you and your golden eyes
in such a short while.

The Psychic String of a Kite

Tonight, love is falling from the sky
in big wavering blobs of bright stars,
planets glowing, pulsing.
The swath of the Milky Way
paints a streak across forever,
not our considered eternity,
but just here, now.
I cry juicy, joyous tears
to be alive one more time under night,
reaching out with my eyes
into the abyss
of swirling jet-black night,
moonless, yet bright above.
September squeezes out
one last hurrah of summer,
of shorts, and swimming and sandals.
We say goodbye to the close sun
and find light in firesides,
and the brilliant stars we fly as kites.

Date Night

The sun just went down tickled pink.
Tomorrow, an ice rink will form on the pond.
Coming up on midnight,
this evening waxes in a high wind,
etches patterns on my glass
with sand blown all the way
from last summer's beach.

Did I wear the day away
with my hard-fought sanity?
White knuckles firmly affixed
around the stems of wilted roses.
I tried so hard to be understood;
my garbled thoughts rolling like marbles
around my filtered tongue.

Your honey and lemons lift my spirits,
shock my jaw with pungent and sweet.
We are okay just for now,
and that's all it needs to be.
We bask in the hammock
with two cats and a blanket.
This night is the keeper
of tomorrow's promises.

Unity Along the Equator

You and I are going through some changes;
flickering fiction leaping off pages.
You have felt the north star shifting,
felt your long-held beliefs
fade in real-time.
And you step up to the altar,
smell the incense, oily and tender,
and know you hold the covenant
of tomorrow's garden.
I slip like ice,
between and circling,
so things don't cling.
I think I have a steep ascent
to my mental mountainside;
a learning curve that is more of a cliff
when people try to climb.
And then I smile and scoop up
some of your ultra-cool,
take a deep breath
of your fresh cleverness.
Then, I set it all free on the breeze,
making wishes on flying seeds.

Midnight

You are a song,
a melody playing through my psyche.
I try to learn the lyrics
and zoom in on the tune;
merry, tragic, yearning
for truth and meaning;
gleaning an understanding
of the big picture.
What the world has to teach us
can be found in a seed,
an ocean, a well, a river
running through us,
trees blowing overhead,
the green grass of summer,
and the soft snow falling here
in this moment of dark.

Away

You're making too much noise
with your silent poetry;
Notes on a page howling,
shrieking in grief.
I want to let go
and let it all run through me,
down, and away, and amok.
You and death have made me cry.
I have said goodbye to so many lately;
fond and final farewells.
Where do they go when they slip away?
Maybe nowhere, babe,
and maybe everywhere at once.
Do they come and go and settle old business
like cognizant beings?
Or are they all wind and water,
drifting?

Biography

Canadian poet, PJ Thomas writes and publishes poetry in the Kawartha Lakes region of Ontario. She has previously launched two collections of verse; *Undertow* (2020) and *Waves* (2022), to critical acclaim. Thomas writes about the local geography, community, and the cosmos, and how they shape emotion. *Drifting* is the final book in The Water Trilogy, which flows to questions of the varied aspects of love. Thomas makes her home with her cat by the Otonabee River.

pjthomaspoet@gmail.com
pjpoet.ca

Manufactured by Amazon.ca
Bolton, ON

39306392R00069